Emoticoncert

Also by Maya Pindyck

Friend Among Stones

Emoticoncert

Maya Pindyck

FOUR WAY BOOKS
TRIBECA

Please direct all inquiries to:
Editorial Office
Four Way Books
POB 535, Village Station
New York, NY 10014
www.fourwaybooks.com

Library of Congress Cataloging-in-Publication Data

Pindyck, Maya.
[Poems. Selections]
Emoticoncert / Maya Pindyck.
pages ; cm
ISBN 978-1-935536-71-0 (pbk. : alk. paper)
I. Title.
PS3616.I562A6 2016
811'.6--dc23

2015028576

This book is manufactured in the United States of America and printed on acid-free paper.

Four Way Books is a not-for-profit literary press. We are grateful for the assistance
we receive from individual donors, public arts agencies, and private foundations.

This publication is made possible with public funds from the New York State Council on the Arts,
a state agency

and from the Jerome Foundation.

[clmp]

We are a proud member of the Community of Literary Magazines and Presses.

Distributed by University Press of New England
One Court Street, Lebanon, NH 03766

In memory of Anitra Haendel
(1977 – 2013)

Contents

THIRD MOVEMENT: SMALL HUT

FOURTH MOVEMENT: OF ONE OLIVE CAUGHT
BETWEEN TWO TONGUES

Is it not first through the voice that one becomes animal?

—Gilles Deleuze & Félix Guattari

*

The wiggle of a worm as important as the assassination of a president.

—Agnes Martin

FIRST MOVEMENT: ONCE THE DREAMER

The End of the Book

Once the dreamer
etched the date
into the book's yellow spine

—the book the village filled with waking hands

the dreams stopped coming.

It was the end of the book
even with two pages left
blank & blinking

white. The *Virgin of the Rocks* cover
gathered dust over time,
and the dreams, kissing in dark quarters,

died from distance
on the part of the dreamer
who filed the book away.

Mango Season

Mangos swing from high branches.

Shake, shake, says the bird.

When they fall, we peel their skins, suck their flesh away.

How could I have lived so long in this house without eating?

I plunge a fist into a fallen world.

But the world rots on the ground.

To the ground pounded by bodies, to the ground astounded by fat

trees sparkling, *I'll take what you give.*

BREAKING FORM

When the oldest tree died
only mistletoe remained
to swallow the tree's spirit.

After Pearl passed, an army
of red ants manic with her message
claimed my pillow—

(Later, I found her posing as a sparrow
caught in the highest rafters.)

Mary left curled like a fetus in a hospital bed,
sucking on tubes fatter than her arms.
Only Ida heard—

God help me, God help me, God—

My own death seeks my father's safety
in the twinkle of mosquitoes sequining Crystal Lake.

Do I find such a man in these waters?
Will he swim beneath me like a shark?
Will I squeal in terrible laughter?

PISS STARSHINE

What leaves the bodies of boys with skin
the same as the skin of the ocean

they piss in—sour streams making them
howl so loud I forget how to

know—turns to stardust, loose constellation
hovering back, over my swimming father...

how those stars, piss atoms, rain over him,
as the boys laugh & laugh, wanting

the sparkles to shower more unsuspecting
white heads. But the bright

falling shivers move over the night waters
where no body swims, where only the boys can

see what leaves, never to come back the same.

Emoticoncert

Who else was there, where
a blotch of watered-down brown
surfaced on the well-read page?
Where you deciphered your lover's
claim that language makes visible
a world persisting in undiluted signs,
even as this sepia sonata still
shivers? You know what you have
to do: tell her you too desire to be seen
in the face you'll never wear. Tell her
the illegible pricks the heart
quickest. Tell her not to touch it,
not to digitize the unspeakable
in clicks: happy, saxophone, pizza,
office—today I want what
we can't say when we say
music, when we say *need*, what
we try to transmit in symbols
on the slick screens we pocket.

If Leonardo

On the plank, one string
makes a rabbit's face:

wrinkled & half-smiling
with one ear

perked. If Leonardo
came by this accident,

what would he see?
Perhaps a battle scene

or a dress seam
lifted by cautious hands.

Trying, I find myself
glued to my only

line of sight—the eye,
unwilling to let go;

the damp rabbit mouth,
impossible to reset—

GUESSING BREATHS

The longest-haired son filmed
his father's last hour
without pause

then gathered us around the iPhone
to marvel at how a pulsing Adam's apple
stills.

Doctor's claim: *Pain.*
Drowning in his own saliva.

But we, small family,
can only guess his last breaths: a song
hiccupping heavens? Four breaths, five breaths—

gone. We keep to ourselves
this quiet, handheld footage.

A TRUTH ABOUT TEMPERATURE

Out the kettle, a whistle
like a neigh escapes the red throat
of a drunk horse, animal or man,
alone, collapsed on the road,
crying out with his last stone:
his voice: a burning silver singing
louder & louder & louder
until his maker rushes
to close the flame.

STILL CHARLES

What is shape? What you
confuse with memory: economy of flashes:

your father's mole
in the center of his forehead,
his stack of clubs,
the way he barked *Munye!*
even when she changed her name to Mary.

No, not this piecemeal picture
of a man with corduroy pants
hanging off his broken frame
years later—Whose skin? A belt

can only hold so much fabric,
can only fold so many times.

The Coat

One hour after they buried Mary,
Larry looted her apartment
for crystal globes, Baroque chairs,
oriental rugs, antique silverware—
anything of value. He flung open
her closet to find a shiny mink coat,
its downturned hairs resting in the dark,
and snatched it for his wife. Ellen
saw and tried to pull the coat
from his grip. It's not fair, she yelled,
you took the rugs, so I get the coat.
Larry argued that since he is missing
from his own mother's will, he gets
the coat and whatever else the hell
he goddamn wants. He left to find
his wife, the slaughtered skin hanging
from one arm in shimmering triumph.

When Ida arrived, she asked, Where's
my coat? Ellen asked, What coat?
My mink coat that was hanging here
in this closet, said Ida. Oh Larry
took it, said Ellen. Ida found Larry
and asked for her coat. A mistake,
she explained. That's actually my mink.
Larry looked Ida up and down,
studied her eyes and her ankles,
her gray wires and curved back,
the knot of knuckles on her
pocked hands that bathed, fed, dressed,
undressed, wiped, cleaned, and carried

Mary for fifteen years, even when
Mary grew cranky and spit
in her hair. Larry looked and said,
You stole that coat from my mother.

STILL LIFE WITH BELT

But the mother disappeared
soon after her nude arrival
with the leather belt cinching
her waist. Her legs, it seemed,
were thick with hairs, and I remember
wanting to draw her ass like I used to
draw models in drawing class. Just one
stick of charcoal, a ream of Rosaspina,
and the body splayed across the couch
for what the hand works hard
to capture. Still life won't last.

MISTAKEN SPIRIT

When we were quietest,
my mother shrieked—*My mother!*—

pointing to the spirit of her own mother
caught inside a sparrow

that entered the studio
through an open window.

We all watched the sparrow
crash into the rafters

in search of a beam. My mother
left her place in the circle

to shoo the bird into sunlight, flinging
every window wider than we

thought possible. But what
if the spirit did not really need

new form and chose instead to stay
slave to the flaking body

securing human flesh? And what
if the bird held instead

my father's father,
agitated and unforgiving

in all that he had lost?
I wonder if my mother

would still try to save the sparrow
from the interior

that housed the many artists
circling her many lives.

WERE MY EYES

With whose blood were my eyes crafted?
—Donna Haraway

Take this: lapis lazuli bursting from some
church fresco or kitchen wall in Mexico
fading faster than the hand writes, faster
than fog inked as gesture: my grandmother's
blue breasts rest. In the clearing
I see the once-black trees turn green:
monoprint revised; "original" colors revived.
The words of the academy follow me: *How you see*
is your own positionality situated in some local
possibility. Forget beauty. Sight is a matter
of taking responsibility. A foghorn blasts me
back to the page, where I mark my torso's
technological age. Take this: Madonna's Robe
Blue, Yves Klein Blue, Coltrane Blue, Blues
Blue. Trompe l'oeil of the wide-eyed Jew.

How Your Hand

for R&C

waves blue
to fall —   *thunder under the lake—*

how it traces no   thing: Saharan dust

blown by what
it never says.

No Hands

Some people refuse to use
their hands

Two rows of teeth
clench a coffee cup

A burqa-clad neck
cradles a cell phone

One man balances
his briefcase between knees that yearn

—All
these hands hang in rough abandon

BLACK GLOVE

points across the river
to the coolest party in town
where friends & teachers clink
beneath blinking lanterns,
fireflies. I can hear the rose
laugh her high laugh. Black
glove, wool & single,
stains my hand—black index
begs—*There, the other side.*
That's where I want. But now it is
late. All the water taxis, gone.
Black glove glistens in silent song.

SECOND MOVEMENT: IS YOUR CONSTANTLY HIKING
A WAY OF SAYING

To the Girl Who Mistakes Family for Reunion

Is your constantly hiking a way of saying
I would rather be anywhere
than at this kitchen table, *staring into your eyes*,
rather move through forests
with four found men than face you,
sister, at this *reunion*? I wouldn't understand,
would I: safe artist in the gridded city,
far from your cliffs & campfires. Still,
I sit at the opposite end of this table,
blowing a cup of tea. Rosemary
grows in our father's garden
where we once dug, long before
the battle between skyscraper & tree,
when we were two girls, only,
running inside the colonial house,
stealing cookies, building libraries,
chopping off doll hair, chucking
small friends out windows
for the simple thrill of retrieval—

O-LIVE

for Anitra

Bedazzled bird, blinding feather,
I have not forgotten what you wrote: *(Olive*

is O-live; have you realized that? Oh—live! Viva Olives!)—

If I had known that three years later
you would fling yourself before a train
in the last Bronx station

would I have—

Sweet hyena, kalamata, firewood, I took

your wish for granted, called you "sick"
when all you wanted was some guarantee
of one permanent roof, one permanent sister. I,

with all my stories, denied you. No wonder you left
us grasping at your ecstasies, the two black horses
you inked for a bride, the wild bells of your mouth—

No doctor on earth can fathom how
you touched us   soul after soul after soul after

O

O no thing at once
hummed clear of all things

O

sun within a circle
in which you are the circle
drawn black
on Fabriano

Make sure the room has been considered

and the basket rim
and the rice cake
laughing in the light

Temporary Headstone

So that what remained of her would not
come back to hurt him

he mourned alone at her temporary headstone:

No One's Daughter.

Peacock bouquet.
Row of stones & shells to mark

the absent living—

Salem

Eleven of us, stacked in bunks,
find sleep in daylight, as rain
pounds above. No need to rise
and meet each other's eyes. It is as if
we came together in order
to be alone—deep in thoughts of last
night's fire: streams of fevered snakes
zipping up black air, sperm-quick, to
vanish. We witness what we saw
and clean our teeth when we wake.

Well, Spring

One of us chose to die
before the sun rose.

Ran to force a force of no
return. Return, A.

Remember how you loved to love
Moroccan lamb, fast hands, a kissing booth

made of paper—well,
Spring will miss your face.

Don't you know it.

WORDS CROSSED OUT IN SUICIDE NOTE

~~my me~~

~~it's finally~~

~~un~~

joy

~~the~~

nor

~~I~~

~~all~~   each

QUILLS QUICKEN GREEN

—each quill,
that is, but the red one:

vein-thin; a thread lifted
from the king's suit. In truth

quills turn
to grasses, grasses
to jungles sprawled across the night.

The artist hunches over
her canvas. Her dark-edged
glasses slip past her nose.

Does she know how bad we want

her magic,
want to hang it high?

RED-EYED FLY

A red-eyed fly met my page,
considering if to stay—his two legs
rubbing in anticipation,
as a king rubs his fork and knife
before carving the veal,
his mouth foaming, his own eyes red. . .

But the fly flew off somewhere else,
uninterested in my associations.

The page stayed blank for a while
and then a flea landed—

Ms. Understood

To be as close to a bee
as possible seems to me
a fine way to be—
queen or common jacket,
honey drenched, amber
wench, breezily trapezing
between daisies. Never lazy.
I would be the kind who keeps
her stinger safe. Just in case.

A Woman Is Not

a grapefruit
is not the sun
shrouded in red
not wintered skin's
first fleck not
wet from her egg
not moonshine
not jasmine
loosening in the breeze
not what we take
from the bowl
with fast hands
not string not dust not
burn not wire not bread
not sorry not caught
in some small
metaphor
not at all a woman
is not any way
you slice it

BODY, REMEMBERED

after C. P. Cavafy

One
abortion, two
scares, dark hairs
waxed for its first performance.

Oh body, known river, I lie
with you each night. One hundred
years from now with
what? Nile, Charles, your father's pond,

or maybe that lake we found
on the coldest day of summer—B. wanting
you, me wanting rest, you wanting
to float over ice in stark sunlight.

Quiet geography. Skin
like pita bread, folded, spread. Tonight: re-
member those scattered desires,
those bodies from which you come.

On Wanting to Tell A. About the Dream She Missed & Keeps on Missing

Orange clouds pass, shadowing
a crowd of waves.

The photograph of you
wearing that worn out halter
with your lips curved to spurt
some ancient secret

sits by the carving
of a rigid Cuban,
his mouth painted open
in a tongue-filled o.

A., that day—they say
it crushed your favorite ring.

Who was it who found
the note in your pocket
with your father's number
scrawled in dead lead?

The envelope stuffed & stamped?

In the dream, that long train
bounces in my palm, as my daughter
wears a boy's name, a girl's skirt, and darts
into traffic. Mothers play

cool: let the child run wild. Trust
she won't grow to follow her pain.

Exquisite Corpse

She spoke the word softly,
knowing I would not know it.

Afraid to embarrass, she let
the last half dissolve
so that I might be right
to accuse her of mumbling.

I insisted she repeat it,
and when she did I sought
a definition: beetle skin;
fragile; iridescent; for writing

on strange paper
this unfinished story.

X

Once, I was not
my mother's daughter,
and saw only my father's folds
in my aging face.

They kept my true mother secret:
has-been; crack whore; accidental ghost.

Did I arrive like baby Moses?

Yes, they assured me,
only instead of a river,
a hospital bed,
and instead of a woven basket,
a cotton casing from Kmart.

Always?

Always loved, they promised,
hiding the photos of my sister's birth
with a construction paper heart.

Special girl, they remind me,
heir to a stranger's fortune.
Consider yourself lucky—
destined to greatness and hell.

PLEASURE SYSTEMS

There, I, side view

    shoving sequined balls

    inside the chain-link fence's many mouths   fast as I can

No mother in her minivan   parked down the block

No school friends around

Just a light gleaming   wires green

    These nights glittering   in their sudden place

MY FAVORITE QUEENDOM

after Li-Young Lee

My favorite day rests between S and S.

My favorite color is the crush
of late summer berries staining the sidewalk.

My favorite memory is my mother waking us
at three in the morning to feed us
the only muffins she ever baked.

My favorite dream is how I fly over
fields of boys to kiss them, one by one.

My favorite lake is sisterhood—
murky waters turning green in sunlight
and the spread of seaweed finding our root.

My favorite food is the first halva grain
stuck on the lowest lipsticked lip.

My favorite skeleton has two doors:
mahogany and wind. A woman
twists each knob, this way, that way,

urging me to follow the lines that lead
to the smallest version of a Maya ever made.

Aubade at the Edge of Longing

for & after Dawn at Bedford Stuyvesant Preparatory High School

Stone among friends, you laughed,
and I saw that the friends were just us
and my father who pointed to the stone
as that thing we each need, only one. Soon
my body glowed a cornstalk halo
and my legs, two pasty logs,
shrieked beneath my gown. I must have known
how the half-lit wander this earth,
how the stone sleeps in two slits
on the breastbone, how the moon is
around like the sun.

THIRD MOVEMENT: SMALL HUT

Ode to the Hebrew Letter, *Chet*

for Nurit

Small hut
of wood and wires,
old woman
thrown over the earth,
you come hot,
scratching at the throat,
marching between
one blazing Arab
and one crazy Jew.
You make dark
chords in me,
wise, dirty tongue,
impossible for Americans
to swallow, or even write
without evoking Chet
Baker, or Chevrolet,
but your sewn sound
is anti-American:
the tremble of pin
poking cloth, donkey
engine, a mother's
snap. I've seen you
dangle off the edge of prayer,
reeking of paprika,
filament, vein—my family
needs you to make *mustard,*
butter, bread, winter—I love
how there is nothing

slant about you.
When I grow to leave
for softer pastures,
you slam the screen door
and light a match.

P-A-L-E-S-T-I-N-E

This morning, I repeat the adventure and ride the bike with the missing handlebars, my sisters close at my waist. Each time, I search for a crowd of Jews to sell me this steering device. I trust these men together. I don't trust the lone Yid with the red beard who stays indoors, reading theories by a bedside lamp. To know he is home is to recognize light as his warning. We always leave panicked, barely lacing our boots. Only today the world outside has changed. Capital letters everywhere, spelling out the name of a place I fear to write my family. The letters grow like wildflowers or someone has shoved them in the ground.

COUNTRY

This country that I love
razed your home.

This boy I love
struck your wife.

There is no thing to love
that will not harm. My sister

steps over the dying
as though they are already dead.

Her idle foot,
secure in polished leather,

brushes this man and that
woman, and I,

far worse, once left
a needle on your mother's mattress

then told the story
backwards. I remember

the tingle right before:
bullseye caramels

shocking sugar to the tongue
and the hunger that swallowed.

That day I saw your brother
and could not see my face in his.

National

The sapphire-stained stars
became a gleaming skirt
in which I pranced around town,
pursing thick Semitic lips,
popping my head out each
open window, chanting
my motto, *PLEASE,* as in
TO PLEASE, hushing the violence
inside me. It was war I needed
to make real the possibility of heroism,
but in the United States I kept choosing
methods of dilution. I learned
to cook, clean, and mediate.
I tamed my flame with yoga
and trust built from the kindness
in my eyes. My heart
was something else altogether.

Desert Light in Mitzpe Ramon

blanches the bathrobe
of the blue-eyed tourist

I don't like this side   *of my face*

He snaps her picture anyway

His back to the land
she faces   *Smile*   Gold

burning everything

NEGEV

In her search for silence, one woman
hears her father bark at her mother,
Then don't!—two days before he turns
sixty-eight, fifteen-hundred feet
above a crumpled sheet of earth:
forever-married yellows & browns
that fade to waves. She can feel
the desert air crack her,
can recall the whir of jets
practicing whatever movements
necessary to claim this unmade bed.

the sky is a busy market
crowds of raindrops chatter on rooftops
in thick tongues

thunder roars his usual warning
but rain resists *talk*   *talk*   *talk*   *talk*   *talk*
without words

First Word

A man longing to frame a desert
built this observatory
to track the giant mortar's
rosy folds—now, despite all
my praises of the small,
I lust for the unending stretch,
the mammoth universe, impossible
poem, orange half-moon
biting down on a black sky,
night spotted with open eyes,
blinding morning, sand and
nothing but sand. This is the hour
for uncertain horizons, for losing
the illusion that one man might find
a treasure not already here.

SHABBAT

Dig the ditch for the dirt
and not for the hole, as does the man
who wishes to skirt the holy laws,
and whose sons, in the same spirit,
butcher open bags of potato chips
so that no one can accuse them
of reusing that bag
for some utilitarian purpose.

Cutting off the head of a chicken
is another story. You think you can
cut off a chicken's head for its beak
and the chicken won't die? The rabbis
have decided that no such intention
can be true, unless the Jew
is really stupid. Such are the laws
hanging by a thread from the mountain.

INQUISITOR

Asking—no, crowing—
at the guard among the peonies,
crowned with a false sense
of sunlight, your fair inquisitor
lights up. Husk of maize
brandishes your tongue
to remind you of all that's been
crushed by the Colonel. Music
in the garden: a quintet of pinks
rhapsodizes a mania of sunsets.
Do you hear it when your eyes spring open?
Do you find it between the fringes
of daybreak, leashing one world
while hunting another?

ZIONIST

He asks, *What is this word*
if not the evil work
of Jews?

One mother clips
socks to dry
in the sun.

(Uri's rifle
stays slung.)

Back home
the Indians recline,
drunk and quiet
in their fields,

giving us
the peace of mind
to fight for Palestine.

ROCKEFELLER DREAMS

for Melanie Maria Goodreaux

This dream is for the school of fish
flapping their bodies against the tank

with beating gills & bulbous eyes
suctioned to the glass.   Quiet gasps.

This dream belongs to the ivy,
the Pied Piper made of stone,
the jade grapes, sculpted leaves,

the replica of the bubbling fountain
from the Boboli Gardens.

John commissioned this dream.

This dream is for *Art
Before the Age of Mechanical Reproduction*:
man-made monument, manicured
lawn, unused pool.

This one's for the two Daniels
forever wrestling their lions to the ground.

This dream is for the nut
picked up on Overlook Trail
and held for a mile, considered
by its wrong name,
before flung towards the sun,

for the curled
yellow leaf; cricket's canoe; chipmunk's shoe;
lemony memory; canary spine.

Dream, I trace your trail with a blue pen
before wiping your red body
off the white page.

Blaberus Giganteus L.

Flinching antennae and an ominous back—
It now shines a blacker shade of black.

Orange glow from the window
roasts its deep body amber. Light
streams into the room.

I, so much smaller.

ODE TO THE COCKROACH

Trashy lover, I jump
at the thought of you
hiding in mom's dark shoe—

Oh, terrible thing, called once
by a crazy lady *Our Fear of Spirit*,
survivor, city dweller, we all
want you gone—wings
smeared across the sidewalk.

Roach, to love you
multiplied feels impossible,
but I can rest at your feet
curled in death & watch

the amber glint of your body
frozen by flashlight. Let me

tell you a story: one summer
I grew brave, lifted your shell
from a Chinatown windowsill,
carried you one floor up,
just to know I could,
then placed you, crumbling,
deep in some forgotten corner
of the landing, where the super
might see you & sigh, might
sweep you away, or let you

be, unbearable memory.

FOURTH MOVEMENT: OF ONE OLIVE CAUGHT BETWEEN TWO TONGUES

Sometimes a First Kiss Is a Matter

of one olive caught between two tongues,
or a sister's spying eye
behind the wood door. Sometimes

the kissers stand on roller skates
laced tight around their ankles
and hold each other's shoulders

for balance. A kiss is made
wilder by sundown, after school
once every bell has rung

and the ghosts of closing drills
linger in the halls. Sweetest if
a teacher tells your mother

who pretends the schnitzel
isn't burning as you burst
through the red frame.

7TH GRADE SCIENCE LESSON

for David & Shira

Ms. Weiss sticks her fist
inside a dead cow's heart
and wears, for one brilliant minute,

a red boxing glove. Poor
heart, dumb on the table,
to teach us about form:

superior vena cava,
veins, valves, ventricles,
small, empty chambers

where blood once swarmed—
Ms. Weiss's wedding ring
slips off inside this once warm

home—*Oh!*—is it David
who howls first? The lesson
shatters. I love that

what is precious can vanish
in any heart. I know
nothing of gold or marriage,

just that today, science lost
to slime, expert to animal,
term to body, living to dead, so I

join my pack and laugh
until my sides crack and my heart
bursts at the sight of Ms. Weiss,

both hands now deep and bloodied,
leaning over the long gone organ
to save her thing of meaning.

Bagging Breads

In the bakery where I worked
when I was fifteen, I was told
to bag all the loaves in plastic.
Seven grain, sourdough, sweet potato.
I pressed each shiny body to my heart
before twisting it tight, then placed it
on the metal rack beneath its right name,
careful to save a good looking honey
whole wheat for my father. Tan & taut,
the owner loved the small scar on my chest
from a cyst snipped that summer—*Your jewel,*
she would call it and leave me to my breads.

BLAZER

You who steals free bread
from a honeymooning table,
rattling this restaurant, this country,
I know now why I wanted you
the day I gave myself to anyone
who asked in a dangerous way—yes,
you, whose chest is drawn over
in fake permanence, whose eyes
flash no promise, who would die
just to teach me a lesson—I've harnessed
the recordings of what you do
to music, let my body unbutton
as it slips below the lip—
if I had jumped off your hometown
cliff that morning, I could have
broke   —*Oh worth it*

Two Deaths Appear

A sleeping nurse
in bright stockings
slumps against the subway wall.
A Macy's bag presses
her calves. I recognize her
as the first death I've seen today—
spirit lurking in some neon corner
like a lamp-zapped moth still
twitching. Second death
rests nearby: a glittered teen
in a pink tee and too-tight jeans
leans her battered face
on her man's chest. His eyes
dart from sign to sign.

THE COUNT

His command: *Hold out your hand.*
Grabs her palm, the shade
of white asparagus. Shoves in it
a wad of bills. *Count them.* Too high,
she tries, adjusting her New Year's
tiara, to focus her tired eyes.
Her thin frame slips forward,
overcome with trash bags
ripping at the seams, rivers
piled to her knees: ketchup
packs. Bottle caps. *Never*
mind. His hot tongue smears
each green leaf to smack
her limp cup—*Let. Me.*
One. Two. Three.

Tissue, Camera

unlikely pair
scrawled on a stranger's hand

one   to make the other weep
        to freeze a lover's tenderness

hear ye, hear ye:

the flowery angel marries the angry judge

Thirty

At this moment, I am
my mother at my age,
swearing to wear a ring
of thinnest gold—nothing
more—to circle the wed
two eternal times
while the door startles
at the prospect of who or
what might stampede the heart.

Marriage

I married a piano
beneath an arc of branches
in any park

only to face a dark church
built from brick-stained bills
cut to suit its shape

No use

I turn instead
to the two frame houses
alert at each end of my bed

MOON & FATHER

Sometimes the moon
rounded outside my window
as I pointed and said
Moon. Other times
I saw my father
in the same light
and called out *Father*, only
not exactly. Night
became time for luring stars
beneath my sheets
while silence widened
for me alone to swoop
low under Moon's watch,
as I saved the boy that would
grow to work and father.

Kayaking in August

My father's voice as he heads north:
Maya, where are you going?

I have paused to watch a swan
bury its beak inside itself.

My boat drifts towards the water lilies.
Their stems catch my paddle.   *Hurry!*

Someone put a plastic alligator on the shore.
Big signs boast FREE WATER.

I can't stir myself close enough
to drink what is offered.   *We're waiting!*

I turn back to where I started:

old deck run by
two hungry teens.

Soup Story

I remember the cold room where we waited
for the cold spoon to turn hot,
as our fixed eyes saw all they wished to see.

I remember we pressed the staircase,
gasping for a common tongue
beyond the hot soup and the cold room.

I remember the pet monkey that followed,
biting the leg of an unfamiliar guest,
seaming her stockings with blood—

I remember how we each later told that story.

Twin Winter

for Tyler

Was it the moonlight or the mirror?
We sought the bonsai to find our own
love poems. Prowled temples for what
the wise books promised: *Eel on a bed
of rice will change your life.* Listened
for the geisha's moan when she finally
lay alone. Found bliss in the cold,
plane-plowed clouds. Waited & bowed.

ON THE BULLET TRAIN TO NAGOYA

When everything is in everything,
nothing seems more beautiful

than the Japanese characters
rusting in the parking lot
or the steel rod jutting from the field

or the blur of straw horizon & nothing

better framed than the ridged roof,
the telephone wire, the shuttered
shop. I gaze until my eyes

blank & the sun makes me

squint to see rivers flash
fires screeching by
Malevich's square.

I

It took some time to find
the perfect patch of grass
beneath the wild berries
oozing from the shrubs.

And the patch was no more perfect
than any other patch
with its chirps and buzzes,
grasses and ants,
unseen dog barking just two patches away,
the river singing her usual song—

I wanted to write, *the river calls to me.*

Instead I write, *the river calls me*
and seek my name in what I write.

Rustle

requires two or more
to rouse the tree;
to lure the lute by rule.
When rustling, how we
be. Wind nudges us
to unrest. The marble-coated
jay makes *rustle*, then *sway*.

Acknowledgments

I would like to thank the editors of the following publications for giving these poems, some of them in earlier forms, their first homes:

Cortland Review, Ekleksographia, The Feminist Wire, Jewish Currents, Jewish Daily Forward, La Fovea, Memorious, Narrative Magazine, New Haven Review, OR Panthology (Other Rooms Press), Oranges & Sardines (Poets & Artists), Painted Bride Quarterly, Prairie Schooner, Same Press Magazine, Southern Indiana Review, Squaw Valley Review, Tidal Basin Review, Tusculum Review, Waxwing, and *The Wide Shore.*

Martha Rhodes, Ryan Murphy & Four Way Books—thank you for choosing this collection and bringing it into the world with such care.

I am immensely grateful to my various families: Teachers & Writers Collaborative, Columbia University's Teachers College, Sarah Lawrence College's MFA Program, Connecticut College, Rosenclaire, Sponsors for Educational Opportunity, and Frederick Douglass Academy VII circa 2007-2010. Thank you to the Vermont Studio Center, Squaw Valley Writers, and the Rockefeller Estate for the support and space that contributed to the making of this book.

To all my collaborators, conspirators, friends, teachers, and students: thank you for your spark and resonance in my life. Specific gratitude to: Kaveh Bassiri, Fletcher Boote, Adrienne Brown, Nicole Cojuangco, Eric & Zoe Cronin, Amy Finkel, Shira Gans, Suzanne Gardinier, Kay Gordon, Mike Griesinger & Sharon Chuchuney, Rachel Eliza Griffiths, Anitra Haendel (in loving memory), Charles O. Hartman, Anne Hays, Jessica Houston, Sara Jones, Ben Kaplan & Noah Goldner, Rebecca Keith, Pam Krasner, Eric Lovecchio, Christine Maxon, Janet Miller, Karen Mitchill, Erin Moliter, Kamilah Aisha Moon, Dorota Mytych, Alyssa Niccolini, Idra Novey, Dennis Nurkse, Rory O'Dea, Emily Orling, Jennie Panchy, David Rapaport, Hila Ratzabi, Carla Repice, Lee Sargent, Patrick Scanlon, Vijay Seshadri, Rose Shakinovsky & Claire Gavronsky, Meg Sturiano,

Ruth Vinz, Larry Vogel. Many thanks to: Jessica Segall, for your vibrant video of this book; Aracelis Girmay, for your keen read of this manuscript's past life; Peter Schneider, for doctoring so many of these poems to better states; Nurit, Bob, Talia, Shira, for a multiverse of love. Tyler, for your ears, eyes, lips and hips.

Noa, always, for the beautiful-beyond-words becoming-you.

Maya Pindyck is a poet and a visual artist. She has received grants and fellowships in support of her projects from the Historic House Trust of New York City's Contemporary Art Partnerships program, the Abortion Conversation Project, Squaw Valley Writers, and the Vermont Studio Center. Her first collection of poetry, *Friend Among Stones*, won the Many Voices Project Award from New Rivers Press, and her chapbook, *Locket, Master*, received a Poetry Society of America Chapbook Fellowship. She lives in Brooklyn and teaches throughout New York City.